doodle what it means to be SACI to you!

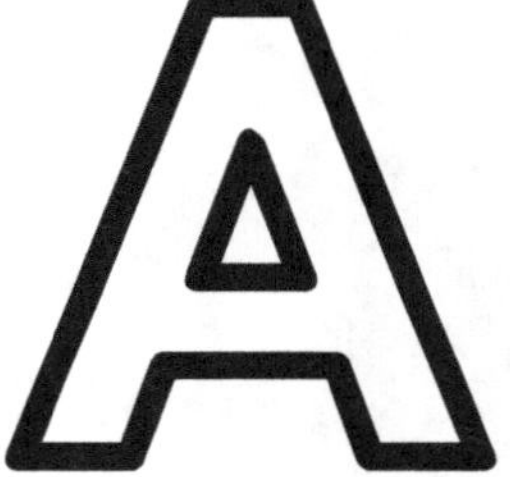

I

Welcome Queens!

Leave all the stress behind and use this book to take you where you want to go! This is part one of your journey!

Be SACI

(A Sophisticated, Amazing woman with Courage who Inspires)

Enjoy!

Saci Culture
(pronounced sassy)

SHE REMEMBERED WHO SHE WAS

SHE WAS NOT FRAGILE
LIKE A FLOWER
SHE WAS FRAGILE
LIKE A BOMB

DOPE
DIVA

No matter how
YOU FEEL
get up, dress up,
SHOW UP
and
NEVER GIVE UP

SELF

What is your self care routine?

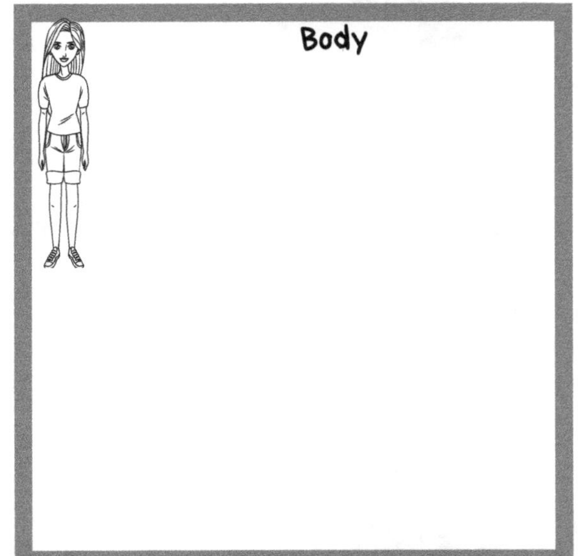

I’M A
GODDESS

BLACK
GIRL
MAGIC

gotta
MOVE
DIFFERENT
when you
WANT
different

MAKE THIS THE
last year
YOU
STRUGGLE,
Sis

Build Until Your 9 - 5 is Your Side Hustle

It is written that you need seven different streams of income because you never know what can happen.

Write both your current streams of income and the ones you would like to create in the shapes below.

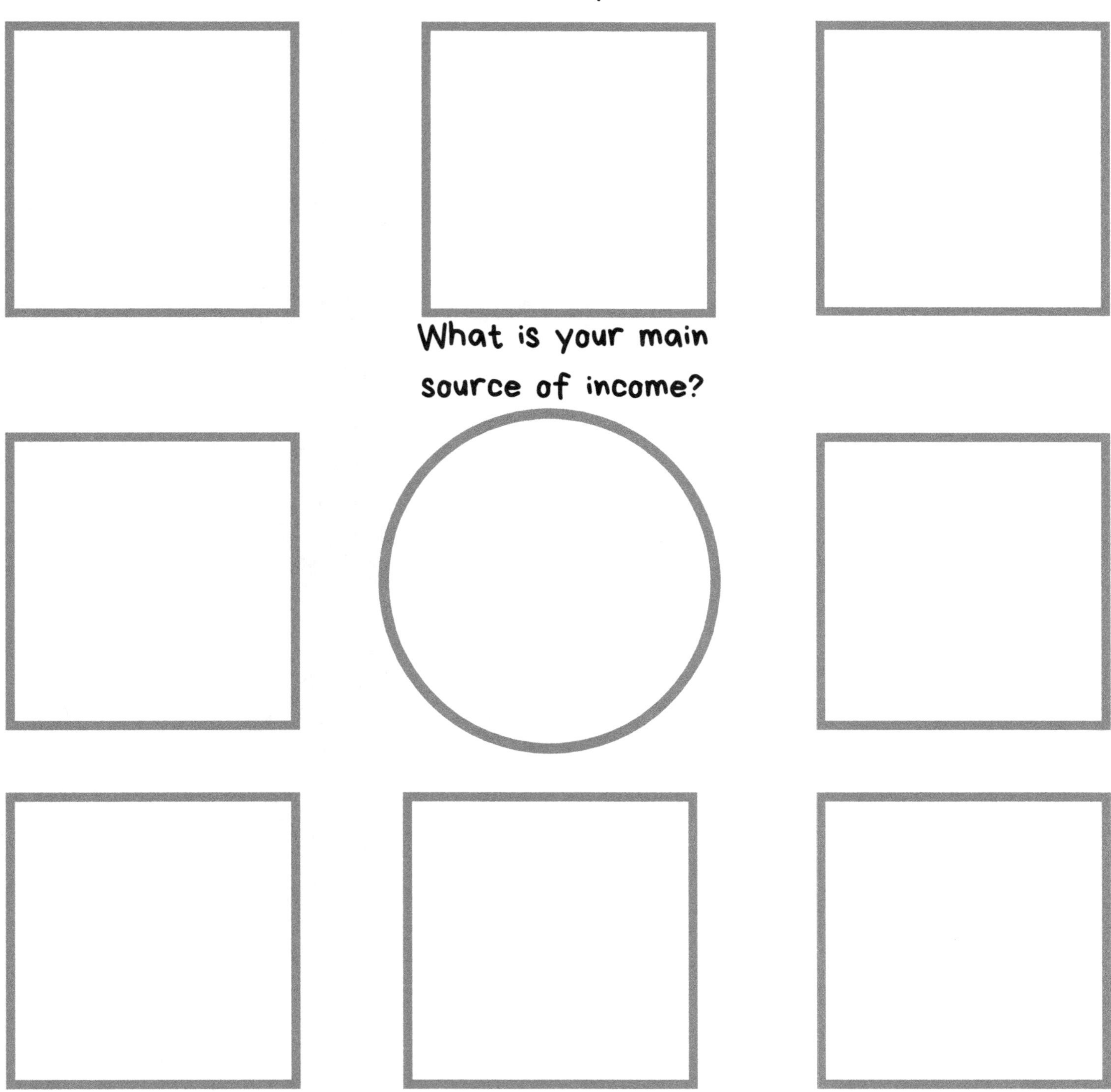

Now What's Your Plan to Achieve Your Max Income Streams?

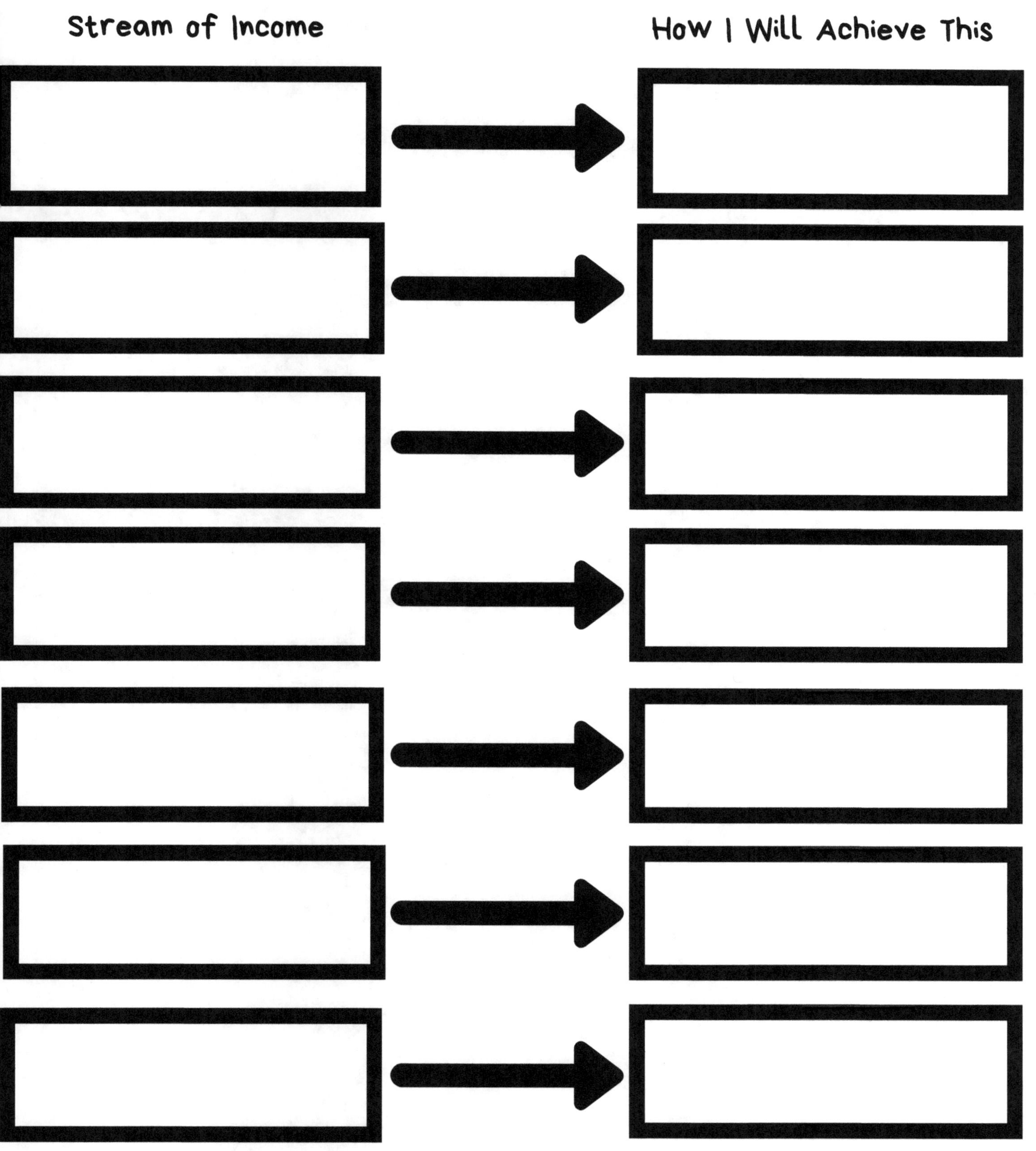

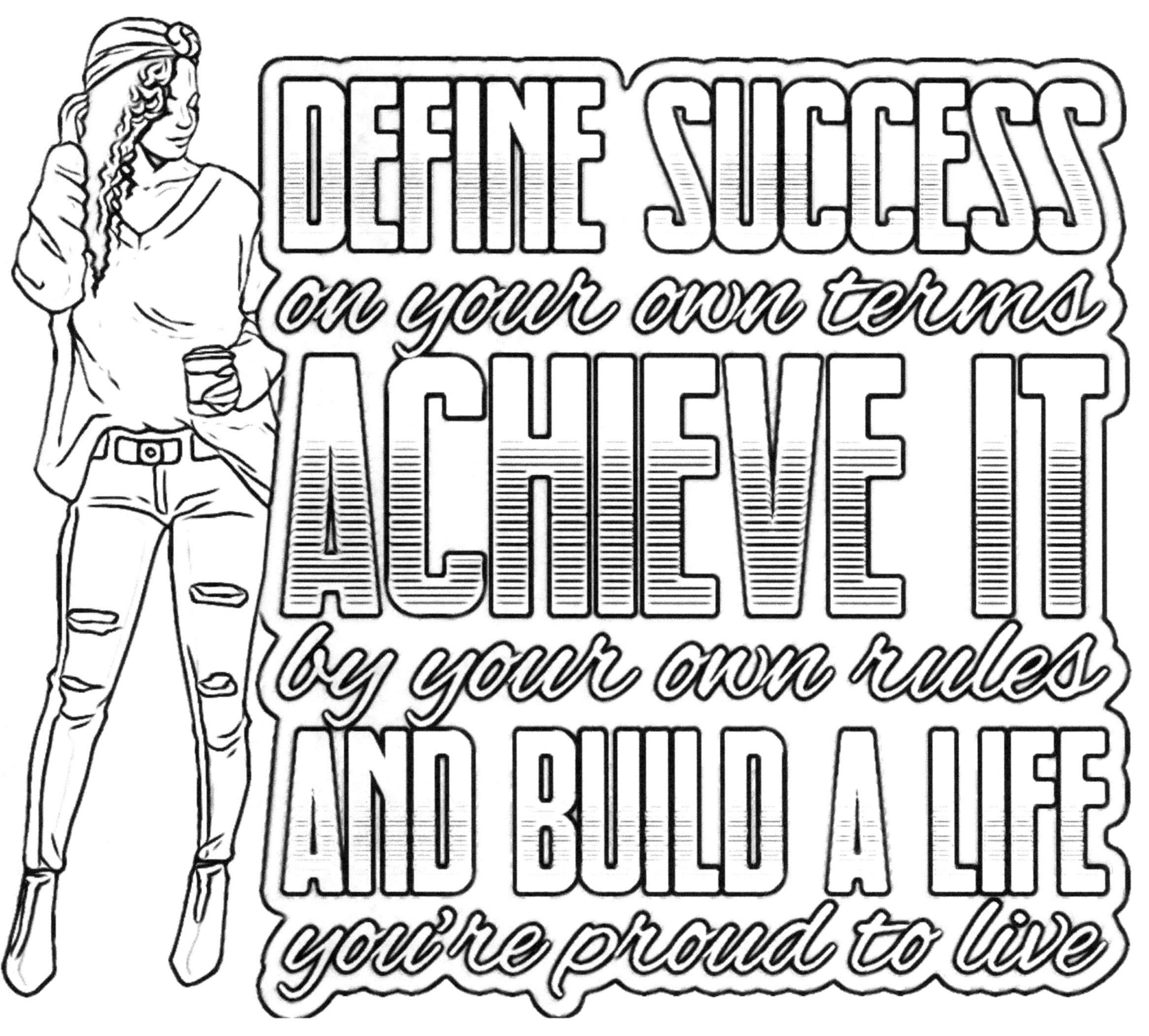
DEFINE SUCCESS
on your own terms
ACHIEVE IT
by your own rules
AND BUILD A LIFE
you're proud to live

Made with
MELANIN
and
MAGIC

You only
LIVE ONCE
but if you do it
RIGHT
once is enough

WAKE UP
PRAY
HUSTLE

She remembered
WHO SHE WAS
and the game
CHANGED

DON'T
DOWNGRADE
YOUR DREAMS
TO MATCH
YOUR REALITY
UPGRADE
YOUR
BELIEF
TO MATCH
YOUR VISION

The Question Isn't Who's Gonna Help Me
It's Who Is Going To Stop Me?
SACI CULTURE

MAD QUEEN SKILLS

ALONE WE HAVE POWER
TOGETHER WE HAVE FORCE

MAD HUSTLE
DOPE
SOUL
&
HELLA
BOLD

Hey Sis!
BE YOUR WHY

Use this
space to sketch
out your hopes
and dreams

www.ingramcontent.com/pod-product-compliance
Lightning Source LLC
LaVergne TN
LVHW082300150826
845677LV00009B/1676

9798663641517